SCIENCE

READING LEVEL: **3** INTEREST LEVEL: **2-5**

new! for FALL 2022

Accidental Genius: Science Puzzles for Clever Kids

Readers find the fun in learning about science with these exciting, interactive guides to a variety of common elementary curriculum topics. From space science and physics to lessons in life science, readers are presented with fun facts about important science concepts in a fresh and engaging way. Charming illustrations fill the pages, and clear, focused text breaks down essential information in a way that's easy for readers to understand. In addition, a variety of age-appropriate activities and puzzles, including mazes, crafts, and word puzzles, are sure to keep readers entertained.

- A quiz is included at the end of each volume to help readers develop their reading comprehension skills
- Answer keys allow readers to independently check their work and evaluate their progress
- A wide variety of activities appeals to readers at different skill levels and with different interests and is especially helpful for engaging reluctant readers

	Library-bound Book	List $31.25 / S&L **$23.45**	
	eBook	List $31.25 / S&L **$23.45**	
	4-Book Print Set	List $125.00 / S&L **$93.80**	978-1-5081-9892-5

School & Library Price reflects 25% off the List Price

TITLE	DEWEY	GRL	©
① **Birds, Mammals, Fish, and Bugs** Alix Wood • 978-1-5081-9853-6 eBook: 978-1-5081-9854-3	N	W1157 ①	©2023
② **Cars, Planes, Boats, and Trains** Alix Wood • 978-1-5081-9884-0 eBook: 978-1-5081-9885-7	N	W1158 ②	©2023
③ **Heads, Shoulders, Muscles, and Bones** Alix Wood • 978-1-5081-9887-1 eBook: 978-1-5081-9888-8	N	W1159 ③	©2023
④ **Planets, Spaceships, Moons, and Stars** Alix Wood • 978-1-5081-9890-1 eBook: 978-1-5081-9891-8	N	W1160 ④	©2023

Reading Level: **3**   Interest Level: **2-5**

8 ½" x 11" • Library Binding • 48 pp. • Full-Color Illustrations • Activities • Fact Boxes • Infographics • Quiz • Step-by-Step Instructions

① W1157    ② W1158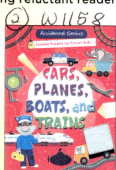

③ W1159 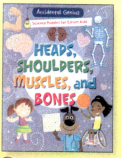   ④ W1160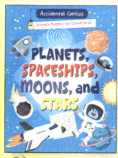

From: Planets, Spaceships, Moons, and Stars

Actual Type Size

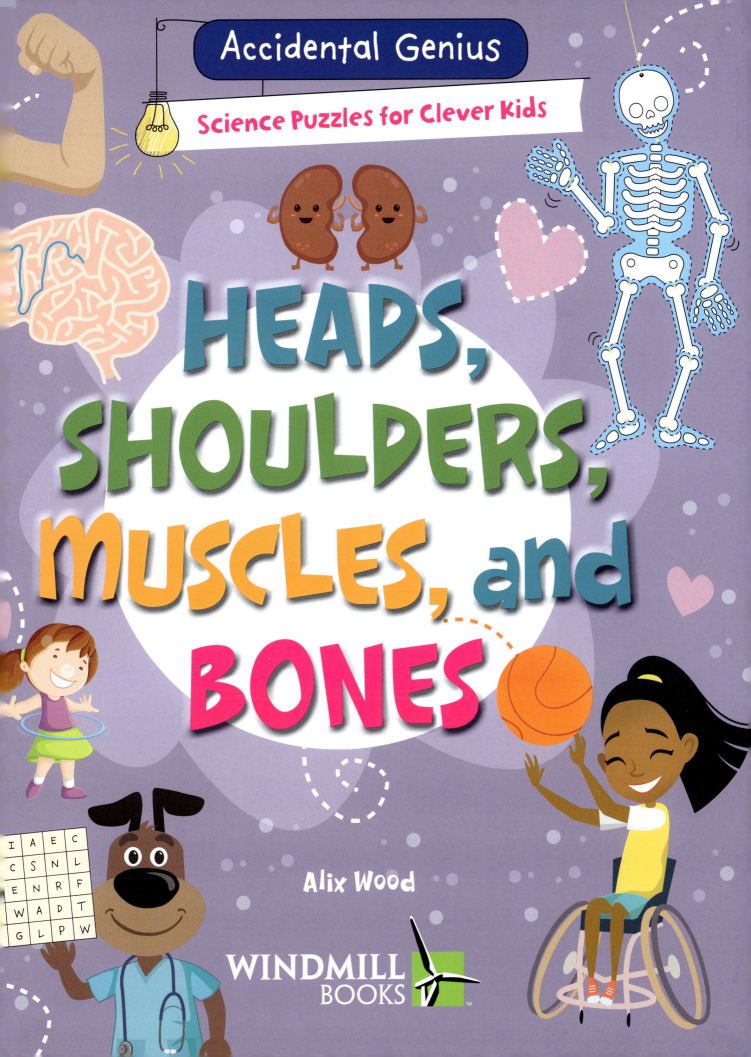

Photocopy, print, or trace the puzzles if you are sharing this book with others. Then you won't spoil the book for the next person.

Published in 2023 by Windmill Books,
an Imprint of Rosen Publishing
29 East 21st Street, New York, NY 10010

Copyright © 2021 Alix Wood Books

Written and designed by Alix Wood

All rights reserved. No part of this book may be reproduced in any form without permission in writing from the publisher, except by a reviewer.

Printed in the United States of America

CPSIA Compliance Information: Batch CSWM23: For Further Information contact Rosen Publishing, New York, New York at 1-800-237-9932

Cataloging-in-Publication Data

Names: Wood, Alix.
Title: Heads, shoulders, muscles, and bones / Alix Wood.
Description: New York : Windmill Publishing, 2023. | Series: Accidental genius: science puzzles for clever kids
Identifiers: ISBN 9781508198864 (pbk.) | ISBN 9781508198871 (library bound) | ISBN 9781508198888 (ebook)
Subjects: LCSH: Puzzles--Juvenile literature. | Picture puzzles--Juvenile literature. | Games--Juvenile literature. | Human body--Juvenile literature.
Classification: LCC GV1493.W66 2023 | DDC 793.73--dc23

Contents

My Body Is Fantastic! 4
Tiny Little Cells 6
Your Bones 8
Bendy Joints 10
Muscles 12
Helpful Organs 14
Busy Blood 16
Brain Power 18
Nervous System 20
All About Hair 22
Fingernails, Toenails 24
The Five Senses 26
Eyesight 28
Hearing 30
Clever Noses 32
Skin and Touch 34
Amazing Tongues 36
What Happens When You Eat? 38
Keeping Healthy 40
Doctors and Hospitals 42
Body Genius Test 44
Answers 46

My Body Is Fantastic!

Think of all the things your body can do. Human bodies are amazing. If you didn't have a body you wouldn't be able to think, see, or play.

Without bones you would just be a wobbly pile of skin! Bones keep you upright. You couldn't play without bones.

Muscles join to your bones and help you move. You couldn't ride a bicycle without muscles.

Did you know your ears help you balance on a bicycle, too!

4

Can you match the word to the body part?

Tiny Little Cells

Your body is made up of millions and millions of cells. Tiny cells are like the building blocks that make up our bodies. They join together to make bones, skin, and everything else.

There are around 200 different types of cells in the human body.

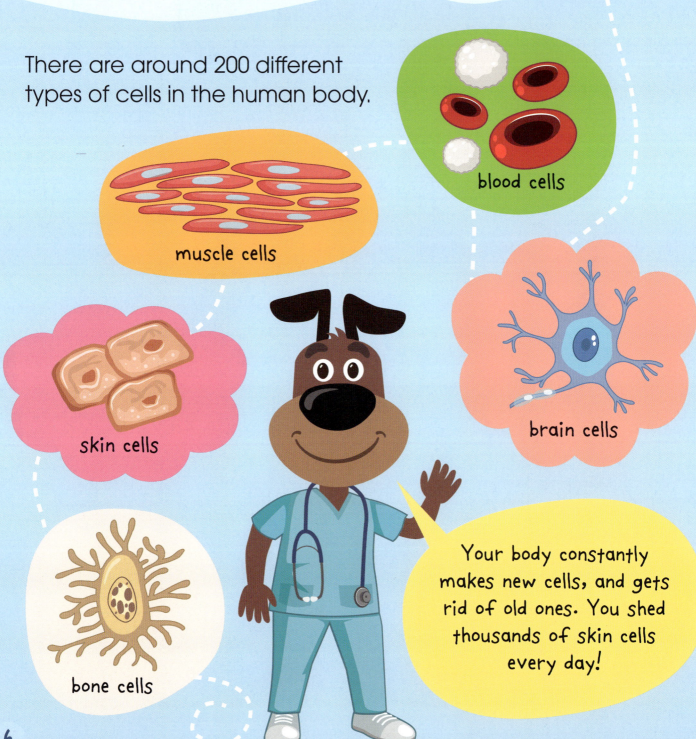

muscle cells

blood cells

skin cells

brain cells

bone cells

Your body constantly makes new cells, and gets rid of old ones. You shed thousands of skin cells every day!

Cells join together to make up our body parts. Can you help these cells find their partner?

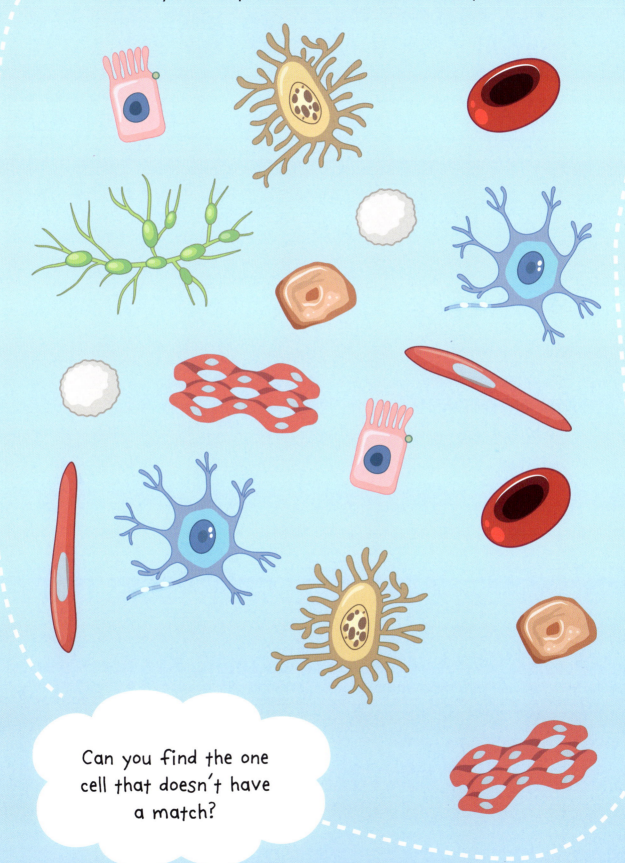

Can you find the one cell that doesn't have a match?

Your Bones

The bones in your skeleton give your body its shape. Bones also help protect your insides.

Your skull protects your brain.

Your ribs protect your heart and lungs.

Your spine's small bones help you bend, twist, and hold your body upright.

How many bones? Babies have 270. Adults have 206. Where do the baby bones go? There are spaces in between some of the baby bones. As the bones grow they fill the spaces, and the bones join together.

The body's longest bone is the femur, or thigh bone.

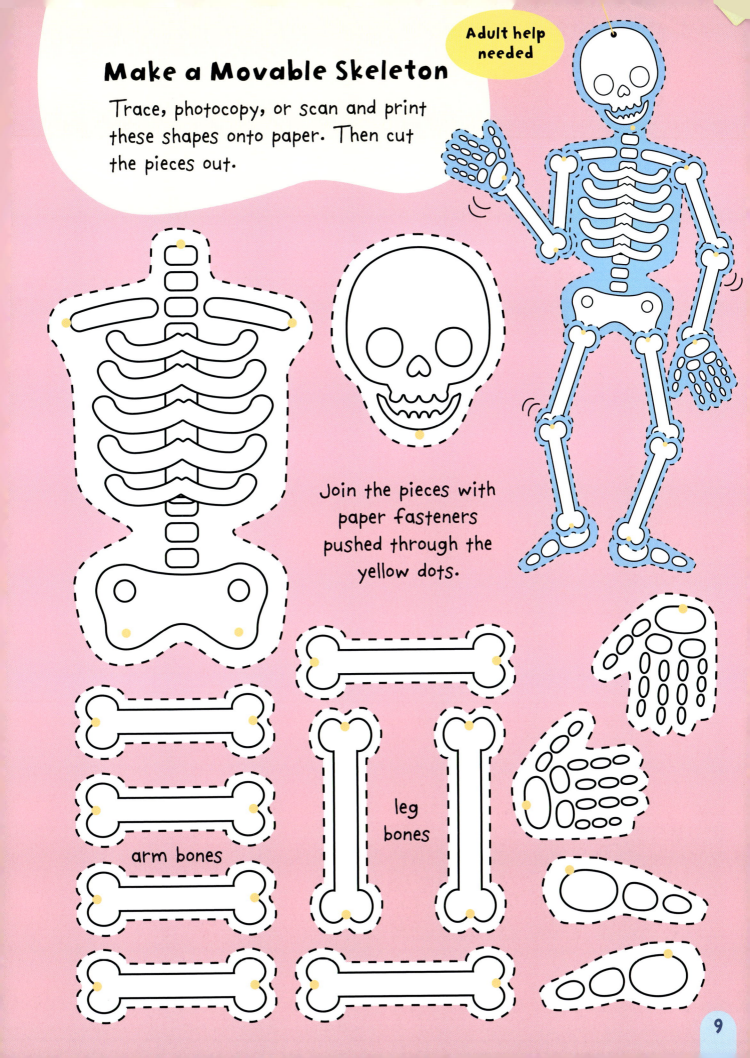

Bendy Joints

Joints are where bones meet. Your knees, elbows, shoulders, and hips are all joints. They allow our skeleton to move. If you made the paper skeleton on page 9, each paper fastener would be a joint.

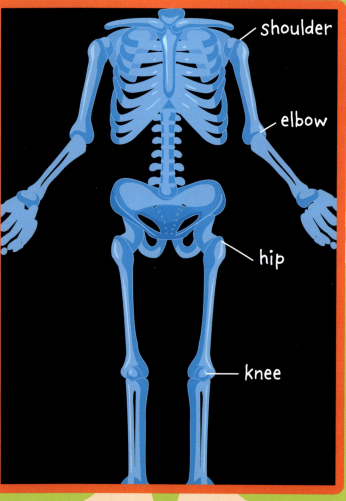

Word Scramble

What are the two joints below called? Unscramble the jumbled words to find out.

1)  KNALE

2)  SIWRT

Did you know? There are over 200 joints in the human body!

Do a Bendy Joint Dance

Joints help you run, play, and dance. Try this bendy dance, or make up your own.

Wave your arms above your shoulders.
Bend your knees. Bend your knees.
Bend your right elbow.
Bend your left elbow.
Wiggle your hips three times.

Make a Working Jointed Hand

You will need: drinking straws, string, tape, card stock, a pencil, scissors.

1. Draw around a large hand onto some card stock.
2. Cut out the hand.
3. Cut the straws into 14 small sections. Tape three straw pieces onto each finger. Tape two onto the thumb. Leave a good gap between each piece, so your fingers can bend.
4. Tape five longer straw pieces on the hand.
5. Tape a length of string to the top of each finger.
6. Thread each string through a finger and its hand straw.

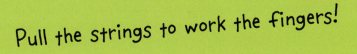

Pull the strings to work the fingers!

Muscles

Our muscles help our bodies move. We have over 600 muscles! Some muscles are attached to our bones. To make our bones move, the muscles work in pairs.

tricep

bicep

arm bones

tendons join muscle to bones

To lift your arm like in the picture above, your bicep muscle tightens. At the same time, your tricep muscle relaxes. Try it.

Some muscles work without us having to tell them to. Our heart is a powerful muscle that beats when it tightens and relaxes. We don't need to tell our heart to beat, it does it on its own.

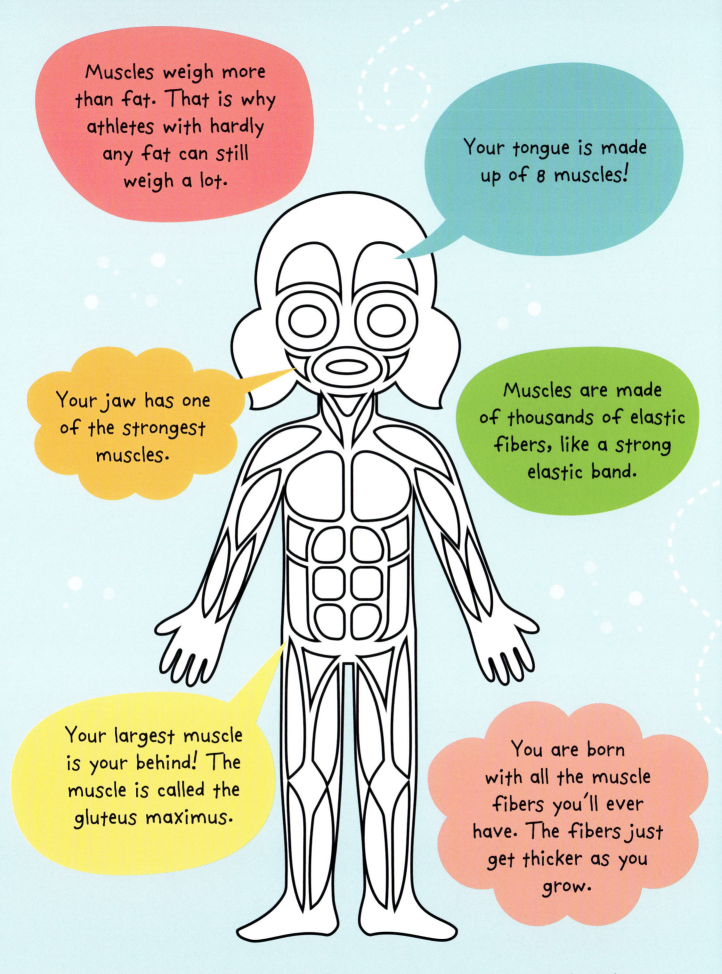

Helpful Organs

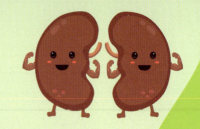

Inside your body there are lots of hardworking organs. Organs are parts of our body that do a particular task. They all have different, very important jobs.

Your heart
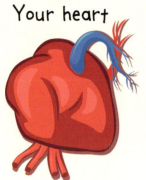
Your heart is a strong muscle that pumps blood around your body.

Your lungs
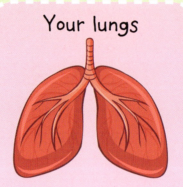
Your lungs allow you to breathe in fresh air. Then they breathe out stale air.

Your brain
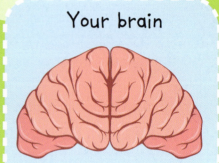
The brain is like a computer that controls your body's functions.

Your liver
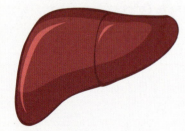
The liver is very busy. It cleans your blood. Your liver also helps break down food and store energy.

Your kidneys
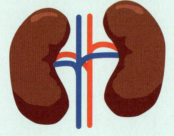
Kidneys take waste from your blood. Then they mix the waste with water to make the urine that you pee.

Your stomach
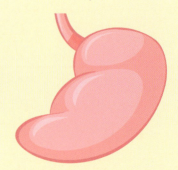
Your stomach mashes the mouthfuls of food you have swallowed into smaller pieces.

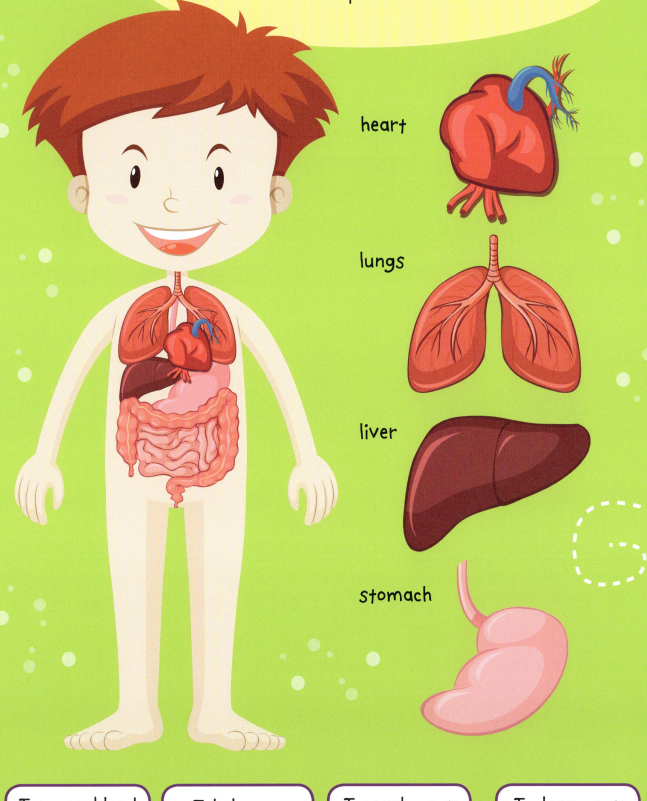

Can you find these organs in the boy's body? Then match them to the right description below.

- heart
- lungs
- liver
- stomach

| I pump blood around | I help you breathe | I mash your food | I clean your blood |

Busy Blood

Your heart pumps blood around your body. Blood flows through tubes called blood vessels.

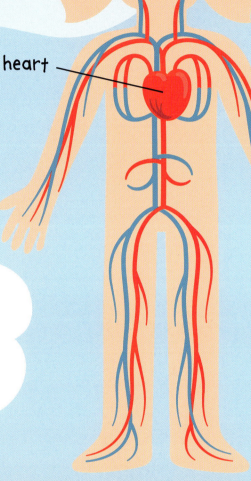

Your blood carries food, water, and oxygen. It takes them to any cells that need them. It clears away waste and kills germs, too.

When resting, your heart beats slowly. When you exercise, your heart beats faster to get more oxygen to your muscles.

Make a Heartbeat Checker

You will need: marshmallow, toothpick

1. Push one end of a toothpick into the marshmallow.
2. Rest your arm, palm up, on a table. Place the marshmallow on your wrist. The toothpick should wobble in time with your heartbeat!

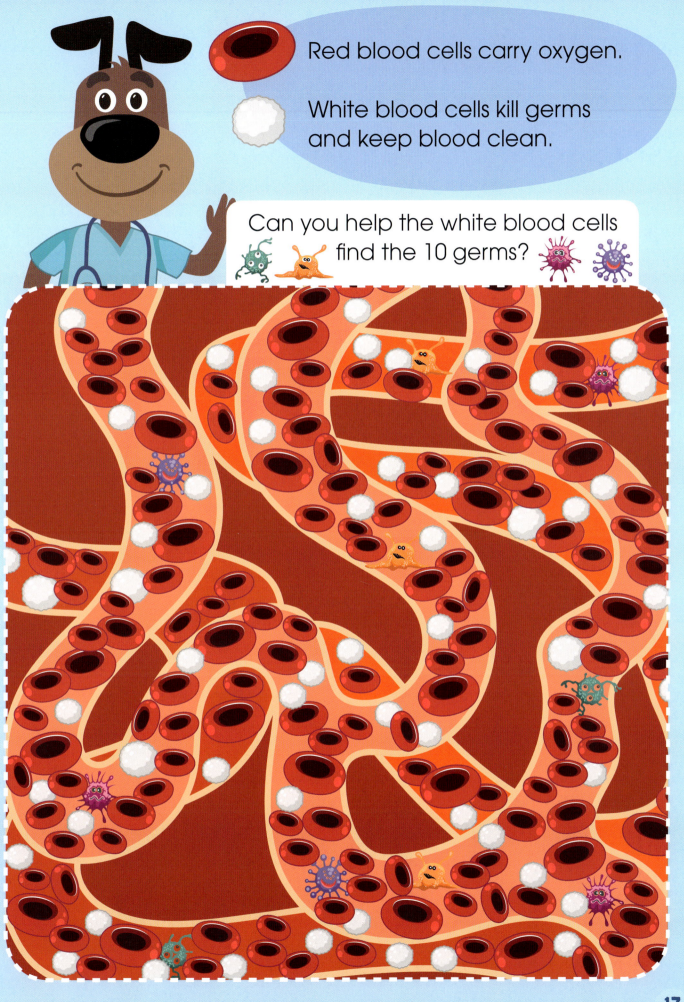

Brain Power

Your brain is like a superpowerful computer. It controls what you think and know, and how you move. Different parts of your brain control different things.

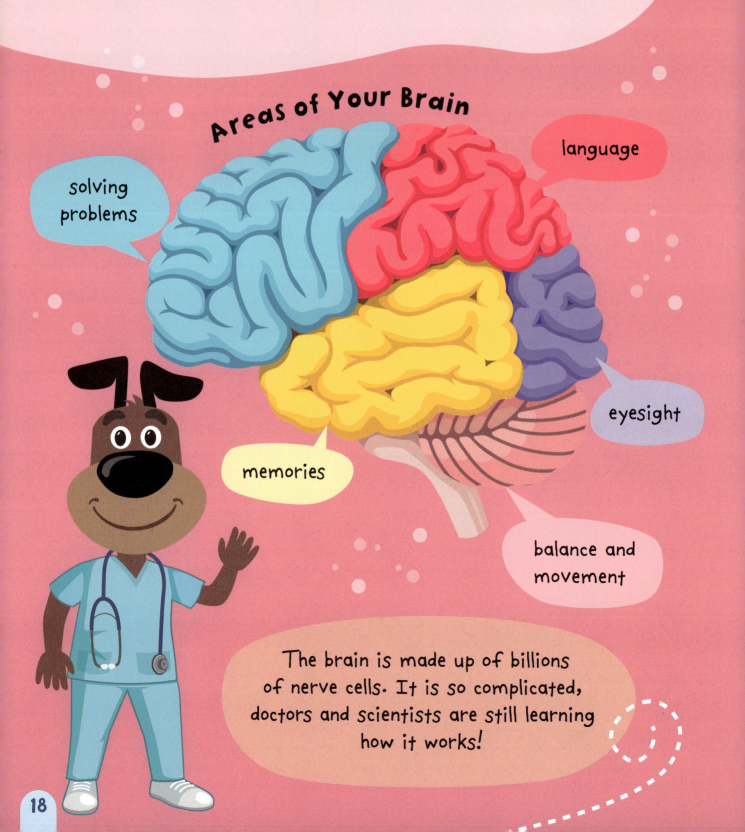

Areas of Your Brain

- solving problems
- language
- memories
- eyesight
- balance and movement

The brain is made up of billions of nerve cells. It is so complicated, doctors and scientists are still learning how it works!

Brain Maze

Help this brain cell find its way through the brain maze!

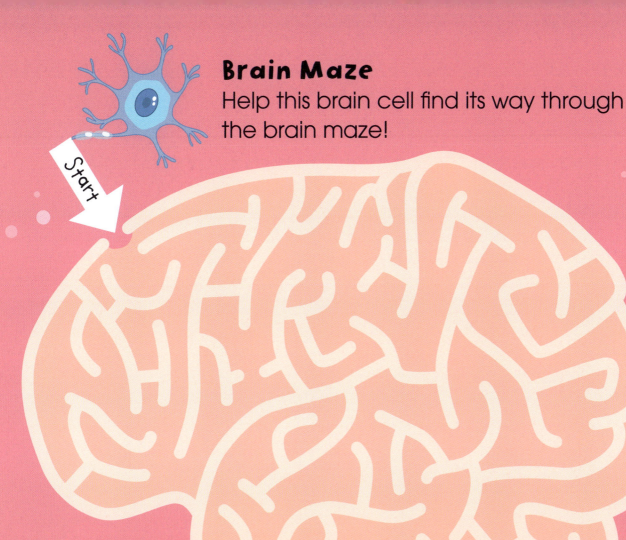

Exercise Helps Your Brain

Your body makes a special chemical after a workout. The chemical makes your brain work better. Try it. Next time you are stuck on a puzzle, do some exercise. Did your brain work better?

Nervous System

Your brain, spinal cord, and nerves are known as your nervous system. Your nervous system sends signals all around your body. It helps you sense things, move, and even breathe!

Your spinal cord carries messages to and from your brain. It's protected by bones in your spine.

Miles (kms) of nerves carry information all around your body.

Sometimes your body needs to move fast. If you touch something hot, your nerves don't have time to tell your brain! These quick movements are called reflexes.

Test Your Reflexes

You will need: a dimly lit room, a mirror

Your eyes use reflexes to protect themselves. Go to a dimly lit room. After a few minutes, look in the mirror. Look at the size of your pupils. Turn the light on. Look at the size of the pupils now. Have they changed? Eyes protect themselves quickly from too much light by making the pupils smaller.

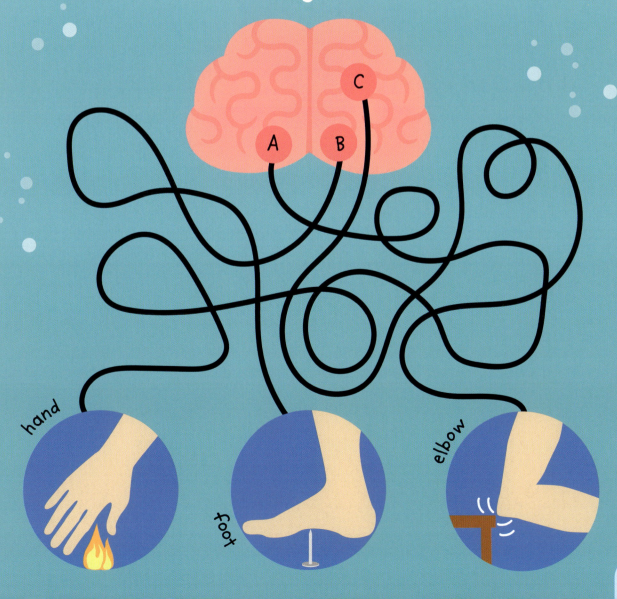

Follow each signal to the brain

All About Hair

Did you know 95 percent of your body is covered in hair? Only your lips, palms and the soles of your feet are hairless!

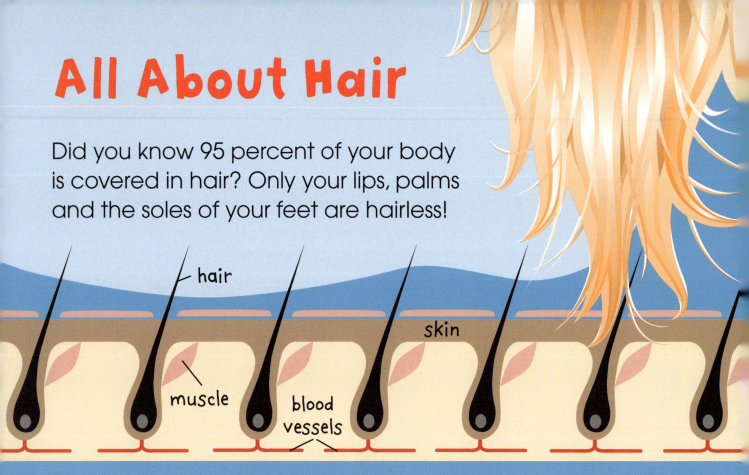

How Body Hair Keeps You Warm

You will need: a bowl of ice water, a friend

1. Ask a friend to dribble some icy cold water down the back of your neck. Watch your arms.
2. As the ice water hits your neck, tiny bumps should appear on your arms. These are goosebumps or chill bumps. Tickling the back of your neck with a feather can give you goosebumps, too.

Muscles attached to each hair make your hair stand up. The trapped air under the hairs warms your skin.

Have you ever seen an angry cat? Their hair stands on end to make them look bigger and scarier to an enemy!

Copy and create some crazy hairstyles!

Draw your hair designs onto tracing paper, not this page.

Eyebrow hair helps protect your eyes from dirt. They help show your mood, too. Can you tell what mood each of these kids is in?

| happy | sad | angry | surprised |

Fingernails, Toenails

Your nails are the hard part at the tip of your fingers and toes. Like your hair, your nails grow all the time. It takes 3 to 6 months to regrow a whole fingernail. Toenails grow four times slower.

The tip of our nails protects our fingertips. This is the part we can cut or file.

We use our fingernails like a tool. They help us grip things and scratch things.

Did you know your nails start growing before you are even born!

Special skin cells under your nail and cuticle produce the fingernail or toenail.

This moon-shaped area is called the lunula. Lunula means little moon in Latin.

This small ribbon of skin is called the cuticle. It helps stop germs from getting into the growing nail underneath.

Most animals have claws. Claws are useful for digging and climbing trees. Humans, apes, and monkeys have nails instead. Nails are useful for picking things up.

Pretend Nail Salon

You will need: card stock, markers or nail polish

1. On some card stock, draw around your hands and feet using a marker.
2. Carefully color in the nails using markers or nail polish. Can you think up some funky colors or designs?

You could cut out the hands and feet once the polish has dried.

IMPORTANT – Nail polish stains! Ask permission, wear old clothes, and cover surfaces if you use it.

The Five Senses

You learn about the world through your five senses. The senses are sight, smell, touch, taste, and hearing. Messages are sent from your senses to your brain through nerves in your body.

hearing
You hear with your ears.

sight
You see with your eyes.

smell
You smell with your nose.

taste
You taste with your tongue.

touch
You touch with your skin.

Did you know you have two other senses? A sense of balance, and a sense of where your body is in space.

Match the picture to the right sense.

Word Search

Find the ten sense words.

- SIGHT
- HEARING
- TASTE
- TOUCH
- SMELL
- EYES
- NOSE
- TONGUE
- EARS
- SKIN

M	W	A	T	Z	E	A	R	S	P
J	H	E	A	R	I	N	G	E	M
O	S	Q	S	T	R	I	R	Y	E
W	P	A	T	V	Y	K	M	E	S
I	S	K	E	O	F	S	N	S	P
T	F	A	U	L	U	L	H	R	T
H	P	J	L	N	R	C	M	Y	S
G	W	E	I	H	G	N	H	L	A
I	M	X	O	T	O	N	G	U	E
S	W	Q	N	O	S	E	N	A	Y

27

Eyesight

Your eyes work hard all day giving you information about the world. They send the information to your brain, so your brain knows what's going on around you.

Did you know your eyes send an upside-down picture to your brain? Your brain then turns it right side up!

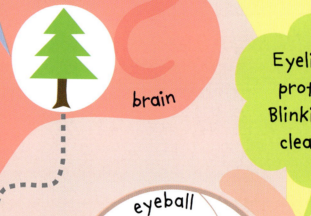

brain

Eyelids and lashes protect the eyes. Blinking keeps eyes clean and moist.

A nerve in the back of your eye carries messages to your brain.

eyeball

Your eyeball is about the size of a Ping-Pong ball.

Upside Down!

Our brain turns everything we see the right way up. Which of the upside-down shapes below matches this picture? Can you work it out without turning the book upside down?

a   b   c

Crossout Puzzle

Cross out any letters that appear twice in the grid below. Write each letter that only appears once in a circle. Unscramble the letters to find a word to do with eyes.

29

Hearing

Ears are specially shaped to catch noise. Noise travels in invisible waves created by air wobbling, or "vibrating."

Make a Vibrating Guitar

You will need: a shoebox, scissors, some rubber bands, two pencils

1. Cut an orange-sized hole in the center of a shoebox lid. You may need adult help.
2. Put the lid on the box. Stretch the rubber bands around the box and lid.
3. Slide a pencil under the rubber bands on each side of the hole.
4. Now pluck the strings and play a tune.

Plucking a string makes it vibrate. This makes the air around it vibrate. Then the air inside your ear vibrates too.

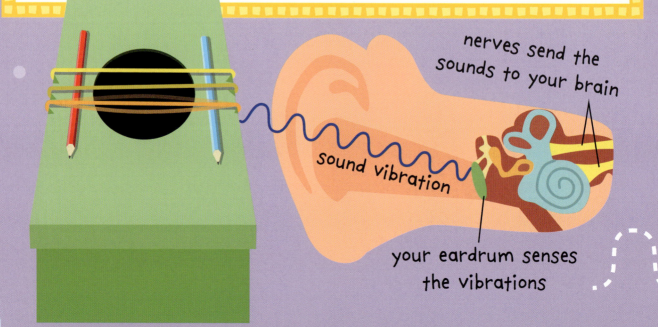

nerves send the sounds to your brain

sound vibration

your eardrum senses the vibrations

Clever Noses

Smells are carried by tiny invisible particles floating in the air. When you sniff, more particles enter your nose, so the smell is stronger. Your nose sends information about the smell to your brain.

Taste Experiment

Your sense of smell helps your sense of taste. Hold your nose and put a jellybean on your tongue. It may taste sweet, but you probably can't guess the flavor. Unblock your nose. Now can you taste the flavor?

Your sense of smell helps keep you alive. How? Smell can help you sense danger. If you smell smoke there may be a fire. Your sense of smell can tell you if food is rotten, too.

Nostril Experiment

Having two nostrils helps you tell what direction a smell comes from. Try it. Block one nostril and then try to follow a smell. It is much harder!

join the dots to find where you might put smelly things.

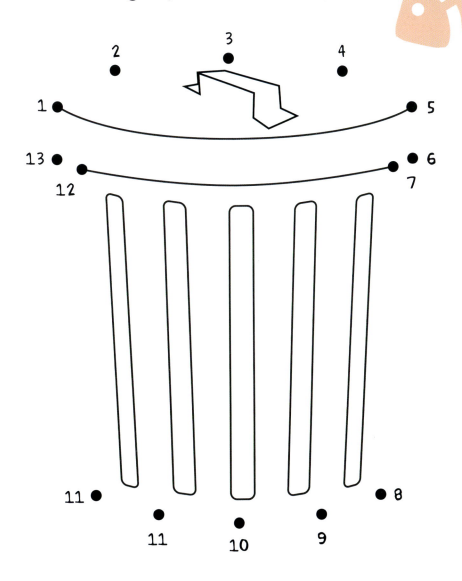

Skin and Touch

Skin is your body's biggest organ. It protects and covers your muscles, bones, and other organs, and holds them together. Your skin is full of nerve endings which help you feel things.

Feely Word Match

How do they feel? Match the right word to the object.

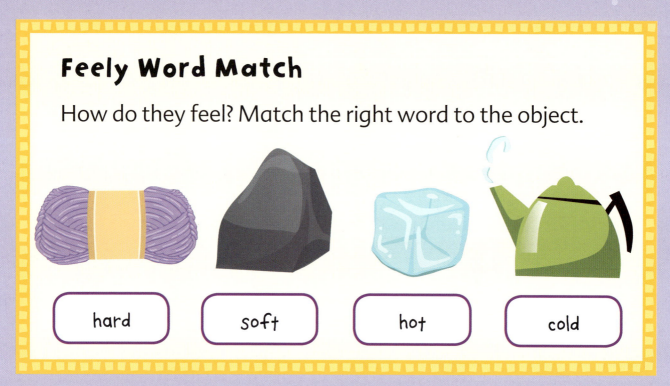

| hard | soft | hot | cold |

Skin comes in lots of different colors.

Amazing Tongues

Your tongue helps you taste. Thousands of cells, known as taste buds, cover the surface of your tongue. Taste buds send taste messages to your brain. There are five basic tastes: sweet, bitter, sour, salty, and savory.

sweet   bitter   sour   salty   savory

Word Scramble

Unscramble the jumbled words to find the names of the five tastes.

1) U S O R
2) E T B T I R
3) L Y S T A
4) Y O V S R A
5) S E T W E

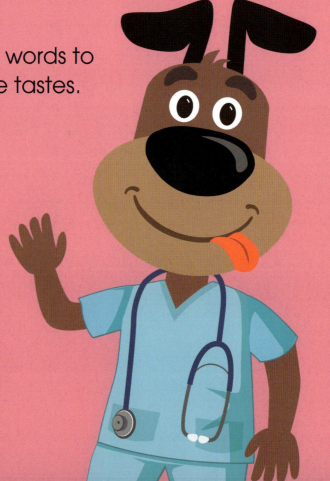

What Happens When You Eat?

Your digestive system takes goodness from the food you eat. It takes about a day for a meal to travel through you. Once your body has taken all the good bits, you get rid of the leftovers in your poop.

Your teeth break your food into smaller bits.

Your tongue pushes food into your throat.

Watery saliva in your mouth makes food easier to swallow.

Food is squeezed down your throat.

Your stomach turns the food into a sloppy soup.

The sloppy soup travels through the small intestine. It takes nutrients to your blood.

The leftovers pass to the large intestine, then leave your body as poop.

Keeping Healthy

To keep your body working at its best you need to take care of it. There are plenty of things you can do to help you stay healthy.

Eat plenty of fruits and vegetables

Get lots of exercise

Brush your teeth

Protect yourself from the sun with a hat and sunscreen

Drink water and fruit juice instead of sugary drinks

Get plenty of sleep

Wash your hands with soap

Spot the Swaps

Can you find 7 swaps that make picture B more healthy?

Doctors and Hospitals

Even if you have taken care of your body, you can still get sick. You might catch some germs, or fall and hurt yourself. But don't worry, doctors and nurses can make you better!

Doctors and nurses go to school for a long time to learn everything they need to know.

A Trip to the Doctor

The doctor may listen to your heartbeat.

They may measure you.

They might take your blood pressure.

Join the dots to find something that takes people to hospital.

Copy and Color!

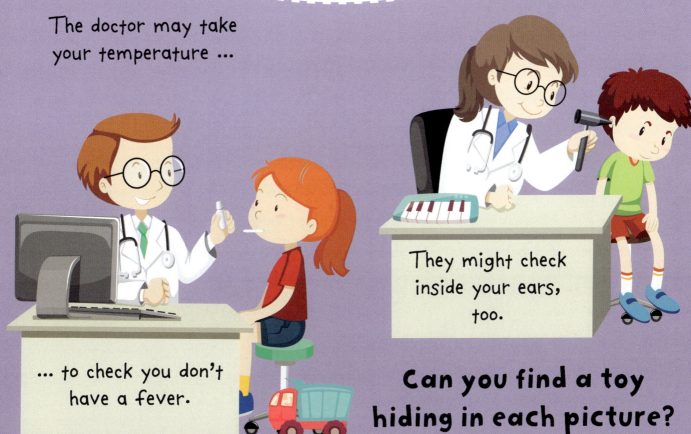

The doctor may take your temperature ... ... to check you don't have a fever.

They might check inside your ears, too.

Can you find a toy hiding in each picture?

Body Genius Test

Are you a human body genius? Answer these questions to find out.

1. What does your heart do?

    a) Help you taste food
    b) Pump blood around your body
    c) Help you see

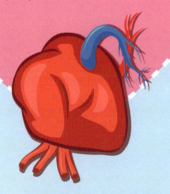

2. What can protect you from the sun?

    a) Wear a hat and sunscreen
    b) Wash your hands with soap
    c) Brush your teeth

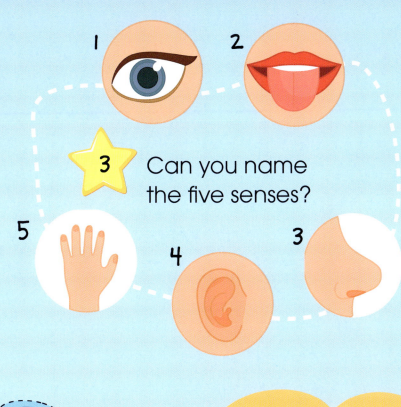

⭐ 3 Can you name the five senses?

⭐ 4 What part of your skeleton protects your brain?

a) Your spine
b) Your knee
c) Your skull

⭐ 5 Which cells in your blood clear away waste and kill germs?

a) Red blood cells
b) White blood cells

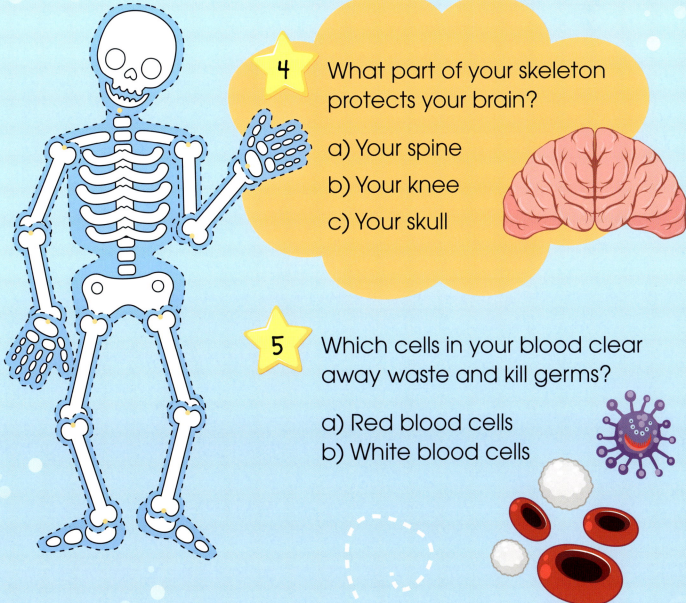

Answers

Page 5:

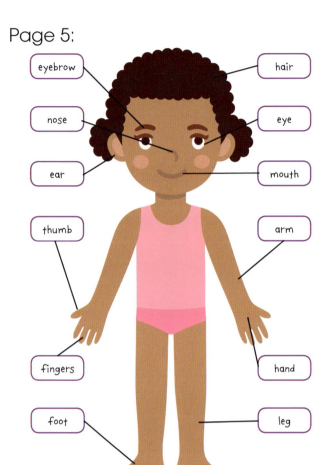

Page 7:

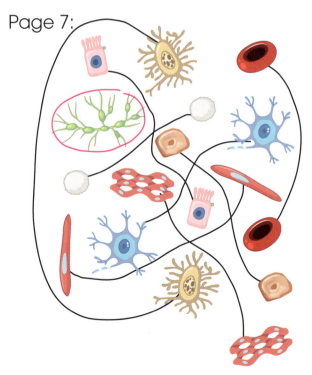

Page 10: 1) ankle 2) wrist

Page 15:

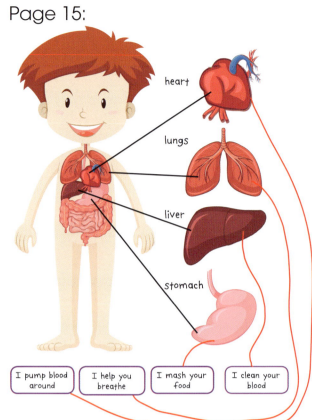

Page 17:

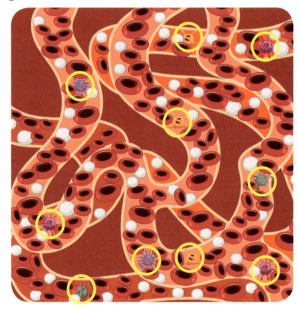

Page 19:

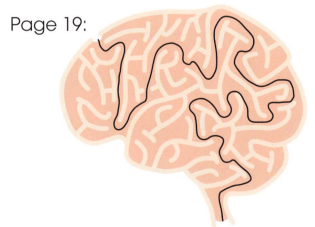

Page 21:

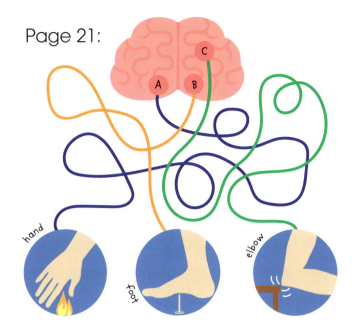

Page 27:

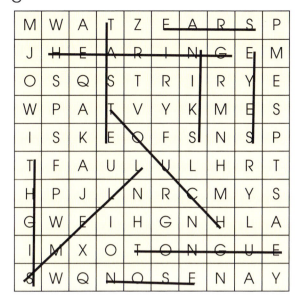

Page 29: c
The crossout word is SIGHT

Page 31:

Page 23:

sad — angry
surprised — happy

Page 27:

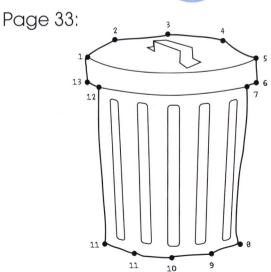

Page 33:

Page 34:

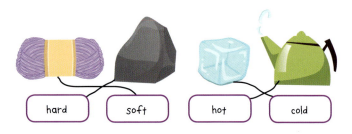

Page 36: 1) sour 2) bitter 3) salty 4) savory 5) sweet

Page 37:

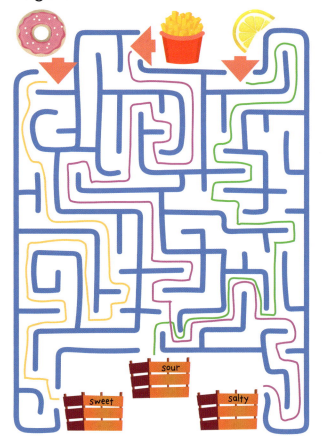

Page 41:

Page 42 and 43:

Page 43: an ambulance

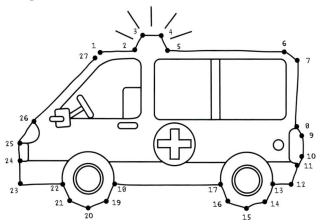

Page 44: 1) b - pump blood around your body 2) a - wear a hat and sunscreen 3) 1. sight, 2. taste, 3. smell, 4. hearing, 5. touch 4) c 5) b